WHAT'S IT LIKE TO BE A..?

MARINE
BIOLOGIST

Elizabeth Dowen   Lisa Thompson

First published in the UK 2010 by
A & C Black Publishing Ltd
an imprint of Bloomsbury Publishing Plc
50 Bedford Square, London WC1B 3DP
www.bloomsbury.com

Bloomsbury is a registered trademark of Bloomsbury Publishing Plc

Copyright © 2009 Blake Publishing
Published 2008 by Blake Education Pty Ltd, Australia

ISBN: 978-1-4081-2876-3

A CIP catalogue record for this book is available from the British Library.

Written by Lisa Thompson and Elizabeth Dowen
Publisher: Katy Pike
Series Editor: Eve Tonelli
Designers: Cliff Watt, D Brown and Clifford Hayes
Printed and bound in India by Replika Press Pvt Ltd

Cover image © shutterstock/Rich Carey

All inside images © Shutterstock except p25 (tr) data sheet, p31 (br) photo
supplied by Australian Institute of Marine Science, p37 (br) NOAA/US
Department of Commerce, p44 (mr) photo supplied by Sea World.

This book is produced using paper made from wood grown in managed,
sustainable forests. It is natural, renewable and recyclable. The logging and
manufacturing processes conform to the environmental regulations of the
country of origin.

All the Internet addresses given in this book were correct at the time of
going to press. The author and publishers regret any inconvenience caused
if addresses have changed or sites have ceased to exist, but can accept no
responsibility for any such changes.

10 9 8 7 6 5 4 3 2

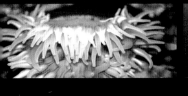

Contents

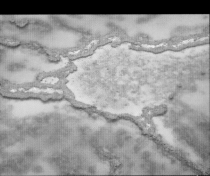

Inbox
42

Reply
➡

Send
☞

Sent
✈

Seen
📖

From Mark
To Allison, Dan, William, Emily
Subject Reef Research and Rescue team field trip
📎 3 attachments

Hi everyone,

Finally, all is ready for our trip to the reef. It's going to be a busy four days. The weather looks like it will be great. Make sure you are all on the boat by 5 am tomorrow morning. Tom, the skipper of the research ship, wants us to get away by 6 am.

Emily, don't forget to bring along the new nets for collecting plankton samples.

See you bright and early!

Mark
Team Leader
Reef Research and Rescue

Marine biologist – job description

It's the job of a marine biologist to study living things in the sea. Travelling to exotic locations on research trips is only one small part of what we do.

A large part of the work of a marine biologist is done away from the water, conducting research and experiments to help come up with answers to specific problems facing sea life, the ocean and its environments.

From the vast oceans to the smallest tidal pool, the sea holds many amazing things to discover, study and understand.

green sea turtle

lion fish

The coral reefs are like underwater cities for sea creatures!

Things are always very hectic just before a research trip. There's lots of checking and rechecking of equipment and lists.

Tomorrow, I am leading a Reef Research and Rescue team of marine biologists on a reef visit, where we will spend four days looking at the current state of a section of coral reef. The area we are going to is just off the Queensland coast of Australia, in the Great Barrier Reef.

The average day of a marine biologist can include:
- checking specimen tanks
- doing maintenance on research and experimental equipment
- preparing food and feeding the lab animals
- collecting samples
- attending meetings
- doing research
- writing research reports
- giving research-finding lectures

5

Why are coral reefs so important?

Coral reefs are home to many unique animals and plants that could not survive anywhere else. Coral reef areas are home to one-quarter of all marine plants and animals. Coral is very important in controlling how much carbon dioxide is in the earth's oceans. Without coral, the amount of carbon dioxide in the water would rise dramatically, which would affect all the living things on earth.

There are more species of animals on the Great Barrier Reef than almost anywhere else in the world. They include:

- 360 species of hard corals, including 10 found nowhere else in the world and one third of the world's soft corals

- 1,500 fish species

- 15 kinds of sea snake

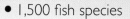

- 6 of the world's seven species of marine turtles

- 30 marine mammal species including whales, dolphins and dugongs

- 200 bird species

The beautiful reef

The Great Barrier Reef is an extensive coral reef system that stretches over 2,300 kilometres along the north-east coast of Australia and is the largest structure on the planet built entirely by living organisms. The Great Barrier Reef is actually made up of about 2,900 separate reefs. The coral reef boasts a diversity of species rivalled in number only by tropical rainforests.

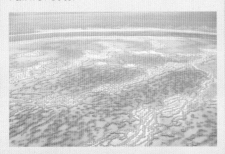

Blogger MB

On this trip we, as marine biologists, want to see how the reef community is surviving. There has never been a research dive done in this area. We want to see if the reef is being threatened in any way. Today, the main threats facing coral reef communities are coral disease, coral bleaching, the crown-of-thorns starfish and humans. It is hoped that the information gathered from our trip will help find better ways to manage and conserve this reef and others around the world.

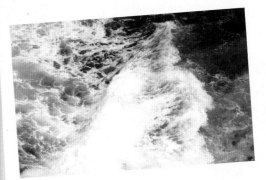

Coral reefs also protect coastlines from strong currents and waves by slowing the water down before it reaches the shore. That's why they are called barrier reefs!

7

The Big 4

The four big threats to coral reefs

① Coral Diseases

Scientists believe that run-off nutrients and sediment from the land, as well as high sea temperatures in summer can cause coral diseases. There are about 30 known coral diseases, and the Reef has at least six of them, including black band disease, white syndrome and coral tumours. Coral diseases are carried and spread by bacteria, fungi, algae or worms.

disease carrier

② Coral Bleaching

Increasing sea temperatures cause corals to lose their colour, go white and eventually die. Reef corals are very sensitive to sea temperatures. A rise of just one degree of average water temperature over the summer is enough to cause coral bleaching in many species. Some corals can recover if the sea cools. However, coral that has been bleached is generally weaker and more prone to attack from disease.

bleached coral

③ Crown-of-Thorns Starfish

Small numbers of this starfish on a reef are normal; they are simply part of the coral reef ecosystem. In large numbers, they eat corals faster than corals can grow and reproduce. A crown-of-thorns starfish eats an area of coral the same size as itself in a single day. In one year, one animal can destroy five square metres of coral. Hundreds of them on a reef mean coral reef destruction.

coral muncher

④ Humanity

People damage coral reefs in three main ways — through pollution, tourism and fishing.

Not all coral reefs around the world are as healthy as the Great Barrier Reef. Since the year 2000, 27% of the world's reefs have been destroyed. It is estimated that 11% have

the effects of pollution

been lost because of humans; either through pollution, over fishing or dynamite fishing, mining of sand, or onshore building and development. Scientists believe that two out of every three reefs could disappear in the next 40 years. We need to protect and preserve these rainforests of the sea.

The Effects of Global Warming on Coral Reefs

The world is getting warmer. Bleaching occurred in almost all tropical oceans in 1997-1998. Reef areas in the Maldives, Sri Lanka, Kenya, Tanzania and the Seychelles have been greatly affected by coral bleaching.

In 2002, the worst bleaching ever recorded occurred in the Great Barrier Reef. It affected 60% of surveyed reefs and the damage was very severe in some areas. Most reefs survived, but full recovery of badly damaged reefs may take many years if not decades.

damaged coral washed up on the beach

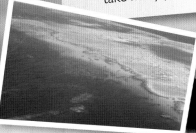

Reef Types

There are three kinds of coral reef: the fringing reef, the barrier reef and the atoll.

- Fringing reefs grow right up to the shore.
- Barrier reefs are separated from the shore by a wide, deep lagoon.
- Atolls are coral reefs that surround a shallow lagoon. They are created when an island surrounded by barrier reefs sinks below the water surface, leaving a circular reef, the atoll.

Top Views

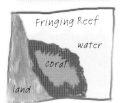
Fringing Reef
water
coral
land

Barrier Reef
land
coral

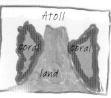
Atoll
coral   coral
land

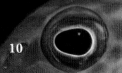

Why so many Starfish?

Why do crown-of-thorns starfish numbers get out of hand?

No-one really knows the answer yet, but one theory is that run-off from farming chemicals allows more starfish eggs to survive. Also, the main predator of the crown-of-thorns starfish is the Giant Triton (a large sea snail) which has been hunted extensively by people. The Giant Triton's shell is a popular souvenir.

a souvenir shell

the Maldives

Tanzania

Sri Lanka

Kenya

the Seychelles

the Great Barrier Reef

Coral reefs of the world

How do you become a marine biologist?

To become a marine biologist takes more than a university degree and a flair for science. You need a passion for ocean life. It's a lifestyle you really do 'submerge' yourself in.

I've always loved the ocean. When I was six, my dad took me snorkelling for the first time while we were on holidays. I couldn't believe how amazing everything was – the sea grasses, the fish, the animals that lived on and under the rocks, the corals. I was hooked! Under the surface of the water was a completely weird and wonderful world and I wanted to know as much about it as I could. I started keeping records of all the strange things I saw. Then I collected as much information about them as I could find.

Growing up, I snorkelled whenever I got the chance. I was very interested in how fish lived so I had a tank in my bedroom filled with different species of fish.

checking out sea life

Conditions
435
Water Temp. 65°f
Cloudy, slight swell
Bottom to
toDate
Time
this Dive
SAFETY
STOP
3MIN/5M

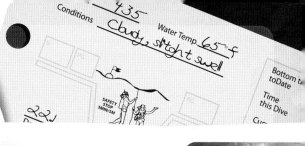

Sea cucumbers breathe through their bottoms! They can also vomit a mass of sticky, white threads to confuse and trap their enemies.

Seahorses are among the slowest fish in the world. At top speed, some species take two and a half days to travel one kilometre! Seahorses are very unusual because it is the male that becomes pregnant.

Parrotfish sleep in their own sleeping bag. From their mouths, they secrete mucus that covers their body, and this protects them from predators while they are sleeping.

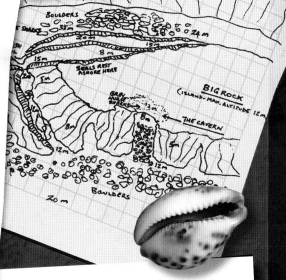

Manta rays use electro-receptors to locate their prey. They use their large flaps to direct the food into their mouths.

As I got older, I learnt to surf and dive. This let me enjoy the ocean even more. At school I really liked science subjects. When the time came to go to university there was only one thing I wanted to become – a marine biologist.

I decided to take a four year degree at Plymouth University studying marine biology and Oceanography. Marine biology is a profession with many specialised branches. The area I chose to specialise in is called marine ecology. This is the study of the relationships between marine plants and animals and their environments.

My degree course gave me the chance to have a year working abroad. I went to the marine laboratories in Moss Landing, California, helping them study marine pollution. This was a perfect way to gain experience and helped me get a job when I finished studying. I am now working with the Reef Research and Rescue Team.

Surf's up!

Learning to dive was fun!

DIDYOUKNOW?

Around 13,000 people in the UK work as marine biologists. They work with marine laboratories, universities, government and environmental agencies, conservation groups, fisheries and fish farms, oil companies and other industries.

- conducting fish studies and ocean protection research for governments and conservation organisations
- researching marine life to provide cures for disease for private companies
- lecturing and teaching at universities
- saving animals and research for marine parks
- researching and compiling exhibits for museums
- writing, consulting and researching for environmental agencies, the media and film-makers

The work may assess the impact of:

- fishing patterns
- pollution
- the disposal of hazardous waste at sea
- oil installations and other industry
- coastal defences
- tourism
- environmental changes, such as global warming

Biologists might predict future fish stocks, to decide about fishing controls to protect certain species. They could also study the impact on sea life of low-level radiation from a nuclear plant.

DIDYOUKNOW?

Marine biology advances our understanding of ecosystems that are still largely unexplored. Recently, for example, biologists have discovered creatures that live in deep water heated to hundreds of degrees centigrade without the need for oxygen.

Who's who on my team?

The Reef Research and Rescue Team is an organisation made up of many marine biologists, each with special knowledge in a different branch of marine biology. The type of research required on a field trip determines the team.

On this particular trip, apart from myself and Tom, the skipper of our research vessel who is also a qualified research diver, there are four other team members.

Everyone has their own role to play in gathering the information and collecting the data. We need to get a complete 'big picture' of what life is like on the reef so we can study and analyse it when we get back on land.

scuba diver ready to go

DIDYOUKNOW?

Frozen coral?

The prospects of saving the world's coral reefs appears so bleak that plans are being made to freeze samples to preserve them for the future. Most coral reefs will not survive even if tough regulations on greenhouse gases are put in place. Scientists suggested storing samples of coral species in liquid nitrogen. That will allow them to be reintroduced to the seas in the future if global temperatures can be stabilised.

Skilled hands required

There are many specialised areas of marine biology, but in all areas you need to:

- collect, analyse and organise information

- communicate ideas and write findings

- plan and organise

- work with others in a team as well as work alone to pursue answers

- have practical and scientific ability

- be observant and questioning

- be patient and precise

- be skilled at working with numbers

- have good computer skills

- be well organised

- be physically fit and willing to travel, especially at sea

analysing data

using technology

✓ Red-hot fact!

A lot of the research may be carried out alone. However, biologists also work closely with scientists from other disciplines, such as ecologists, geneticists or biochemists.

Let's get started!

Bottom time 5·60 min
              38

5·98 min

8-10 m

BOULDERS

Me

As team leader in this expedition, my job is to make sure we collect information in all areas, to give us the best scientific 'big picture' of the reef. As a marine ecologist, I will be keeping a special eye on how all the living things that rely on each other survive as a community.

Allison is a marine botanist. She is a specialist studying ocean plants. Allison will be collecting samples of seagrasses and algae. The reef is home to about 500 species of algae. Most seaweeds are types of algae and provide an important food source and breeding ground for many reef animals. Allison is also going to look at zooxanthellae (zoe-zan-thell-ee) — the single-celled algae which live within coral and help build reefs.

What are you drinking?

KELP AND OTHER SEAWEEDS ARE USED TO THICKEN AND GEL MANY PRODUCTS, INCLUDING BEER, FRUIT JUICE DRINKS, TOOTHPASTE, PET FOOD AND MILKSHAKES!

an underwater forest

What is coral?

Coral looks like a plant but is really an animal with a few plant cells added. The plant part means that corals can use energy from the sun to make their own energy. They can photosynthesise, which means they can convert sunlight into simple sugars. Photosynthesis is something only plants can do.

coral in the sunlight

coral researchers at work

In the process of photosynthesis, sea plants release oxygen into the water. Half of the world's oxygen is produced by this process. The other half is produced via photosynthesis on land by trees, shrubs, grasses and other plants.

Dan studies coral. He is an expert coral research scientist. Dan will be looking at the types of coral on the reef, the percentage of dead coral to live coral, as well as the age of the coral.
He will also be recording the amount of limestone as, over time, dead coral becomes limestone and this will give us a good idea of how old this part of the reef is.

William is a marine zoologist. Marine zoology is the study of the animals that live in the sea. William's special interest is marine invertebrates. Invertebrates are animals that do not have backbones, such as sea worms, sea slugs, sea stars, lobsters and sea jellies. William is going to be keeping count of the number of invertebrate animals that call this reef home.

jellyfish

sea star

Emily is also a marine zoologist. She has a special interest in ichthyology – the study of fish. Emily will be studying the fish populations, and the variety and biodiversity of fish on the reef. Biodiversity is the number of different species in an area.

A marine zoologist at work.

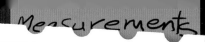

lobster

brittle star

What different animals can a marine zoologist study?

Here are some more specialised branches of marine zoology:

- **Marine mammalogy** is the study of marine mammals such as whales, manatees and dolphins.

- **Ichthyology** is the study of fish.

- **Parasitology** is the study of marine parasites.

- **Marine bacteriology** is the study of bacteria that live in the sea.

- **Marine biochemistry** is the study of chemicals in marine plants and animals.

- **Marine physiology** is the study of the bodies of marine plants and animals.

manatee

DIDYOUKNOW?

I'll grow a new one!

If sea stars lose an arm, it grows right back. Brittle stars, which look a bit different (check out the photo above), even break off arms as a means of defence. (They know their new ones will grow quickly!)

✓ Red-hot fact!

CEFAS is the Centre for Environment, Fisheries and Aquaculture Science in the UK. They research rivers and seas, wild and farmed fish and marine habitats.

History of marine science

The Challenger Society for Marine Science is named after the ship H.M.S. Challenger, which was used in one of the most important marine studies ever conducted. On the 7th December 1872, Charles Wyville Thomson, from Edinburgh University put to sea from Sheerness aboard the H.M.S. Challenger. It was a wooden sailing ship and the guns were removed to make room for a research laboratory.

With the 200 crew, there were six scientists. They sailed across North and South Atlantic and Pacific Oceans and travelled to the North Atlantic polar seas and south of the Antarctic Circle.

The Challenger Society still research seas and oceans to help us understand how we can manage them more effectively.

The scientific findings were examined by over 100 scientists and eventually they were turned into 50 huge books of information!

DID YOU KNOW?

Monitoring waste

The North Sea has been the focus of offshore oil and gas production over the past 40 years and hydrocarbons have been discharged to the area which can seriously affect marine biodiversity. The Fisheries Research Services (FRS) based in Scotland monitor the North Sea for any problems.

The UK has a remarkable 20,000 km of coastline, and our waters are home to an astonishingly diverse range of marine wildlife. But many are in severe decline and urgently need protection.

Health Checks!

A UK marine health check is regularly made by The World Wildlife Fund (WWF). There are now Marine Protected Zones to protect marine biodiversity. These species and habits are examples of those in serious decline:

Atlantic salmon

Atlantic salmon is found throughout Britain and Ireland. It spends most of its adult life at sea, but lives in fresh water during its reproductive and nursery phases. Numbers have been in decline over the past 30 years.

Seagrass habitats

Seagrass beds are rich habitats for marine life and important sources of food for wading birds. They're also a spawning and nursery habitat for many types of fish and seahorses. Seagrass beds were affected by a wasting disease and there are still no signs of recovery.

Pink Sea Fan

The pink sea fan is one of the most exotic of our seabed species. It thrives only in south-west Britain where, at a few locations, it can occur in 'forests'. Although pink sea fans are no longer in overall decline, populations are classified as degraded as a result of past and continuing damaging activities, like dredging for scallops.

23

Equipment checklist

Here's a list of some of the specialised equipment we will be taking on this trip:

✔ Diving gear
  wetsuits, fins, masks, air tanks, regulators, weight belts

✔ Collecting bags
  when a sample is collected it needs to be marked with specific information, like the dive date, location, time and temperature of the water, and put in its own bag

✔ Portable GPS (Global Positioning System)
  this lets you know your exact location

✔ Manta board
  for manta towing – during a manta tow, a diver uses a manta board and is towed underwater behind a small boat around the reef. This lets the diver survey a large area in a small amount of time, and with very little water movement so the animals on the reef are not scared away. The boat stops every two minutes so the diver can record data.

✔ Microscopes

✔ Thermometers

✔ Nets
  for collecting plankton and fish samples

✔ Collecting buckets

✔ Specimen jars
  in a variety of sizes: small, medium and large

✔ Underwater camera

✔ Underwater video cameras

✔ Slates and pencils
  for writing underwater

✔ Measuring tape
  for marking out transects. A transect is an area to be surveyed and recorded.

✔ Bottom corers
  for sampling sediment in the seabed.

Re-No.	Tow No.	COT		Coral Cover		Scars	Cover SC	Vis.	Other
		No.	Size	Live	Dead				
	1								
	2								
	3								
	4								
	5								
	6								

Reef ....

Wind .... Cloud .... Sea ....

Time .... Date .... Tide ....

Collectors ....

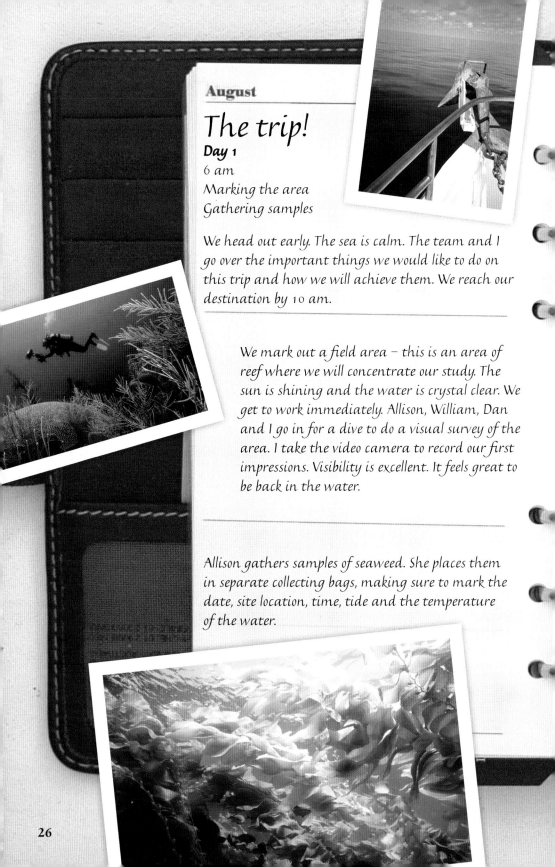

August

The trip!
Day 1
6 am
Marking the area
Gathering samples

We head out early. The sea is calm. The team and I go over the important things we would like to do on this trip and how we will achieve them. We reach our destination by 10 am.

We mark out a field area – this is an area of reef where we will concentrate our study. The sun is shining and the water is crystal clear. We get to work immediately. Allison, William, Dan and I go in for a dive to do a visual survey of the area. I take the video camera to record our first impressions. Visibility is excellent. It feels great to be back in the water.

Allison gathers samples of seaweed. She places them in separate collecting bags, making sure to mark the date, site location, time, tide and the temperature of the water.

Emily conducts a visual fish count. With William's help, she marks out a square transect area and begins counting. She notes and compares the number of small to large fish so she can see how they are breeding. She also counts the number of different fish species so she can get an idea of the fish biodiversity of the reef.

Emily notices that the parrotfish have been feeding on some brain coral.

Parrotfish have unusual mouths with large teeth that are fused together like a beak. They use their beaks to bite off tiny pieces of stony coral (the size of fine sand) to eat.

A large sea turtle swims by and happily lets me capture it on video.

In the afternoon, Dan and I take the underwater cameras into the water. We take coral photos for the coral visual library we are compiling back at the lab. William takes the first of many water samples to be tested and analysed. Measuring water quality is one way we can see if humans have had any effect on the reef.

Day 2

Dan and Allison carry out an extensive survey of the types of coral found in the area. Dan compares the number of hard corals and soft corals. Emily takes more water samples. She also uses a plankton net to scoop up plankton samples. By measuring its abundance, Emily can begin to estimate the size of the fish population.

sponge coral

- Get
- send
- politic
- funds

28

Phytoplankton are the basic food of all ocean life and the foundation of the marine food chain.

Zooplankton are microscopic animals that feed on other plankton. They include single-celled animals, tiny crustaceans like krill and even the larvae (babies) of molluscs, squid, lobsters and sea stars.

Plankton is the first link in the marine food chain.

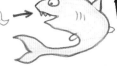

plankton   coral   small fish   big fish   bigger fish

Checking the water

Plankton can only be seen under a microscope. They are tiny organisms that float freely and drift with the ocean currents. Plankton is made up of tiny plants called phytoplankton and tiny animals called zooplankton.

PLANKTON – so tiny but so important.

29

August

Emily looks at four types of nutrients found in the water – nitrate, nitrite, phosphate and silica. These nutrients, along with sunlight, are needed by phytoplankton for growth and survival. Healthy phytoplankton nutrient levels mean lots of healthy food for the reef!

Emily also checks the water for signs of pollution and chemicals from farming and urban development or from passing ships. Good, clear water quality is vital for a healthy reef. Reefs can only grow in sunny, shallow and clear water.

William does an invertebrate count. Sample sea slugs and sea worms are caught to take back to the lab. William's experiments will give us a better understanding of invertebrates and their role in the reef community.

Christmas tree worms

Nudibranches are very colourful sea slugs. Their bodies are decorated with vibrant colours which warn predators that they taste disgusting.

August

PROJECTS

INFORMATION

FINANCIAL

Day 3

Today Dan, William and Allison take the smaller boat so Dan can do a crown-of-thorns starfish count using the manta board. William and Allison stop the boat every two minutes so Dan, who is looking around underwater, can survey the area, recording his numbers on a slate board.

manta towing

August

WK	M	T	W	T	F	S	S
31	1	1	2	3	4	5	6
32	7	8	9	10	11	12	13
33	14	15	16	17	18	19	20
34	21	22	23	24	25	26	27
35	28	29	30	31	1	1	1

31

August

After the broad overview survey is done they come back to collect me. Dan, William and I dive together to do a fine scale survey. We divide the area into 40 transects (50 metres long by 5 metres wide) and count all the crown-of-thorns starfish we see in a transect. We also record their size to give us an idea of how old the starfish are.

The crown-of-thorns starfish spits its guts out over the coral to break it down and eat it.

Comparing and contrasting findings

The manta board survey let us estimate how many adult starfish were in a wide area of the reef. The fine scale survey let us see exactly how many starfish are in our field area. The fine scale survey gave us a more accurate number, while the manta board survey gave an estimate of the number in the surrounding area.

We use compare and contrast techniques with all our research results. We compare the results to others from similar areas and to past results from this reef. This gives us a bigger picture of what is going on here and now, what's normal and how things have changed.

Collecting the samples pulled out of the ocean floor with the bottom corer.

Day 4

As this is our last day, everyone is busy getting last samples to take back to the lab and doing final species counts.

Samples of the reef floor are taken using the bottom corer.

All the samples are checked to see if they are marked correctly. The water in the fish tanks is changed to keep all the living samples healthy.

We all take final dives. I do a final video survey of the reef while Allison takes photos with the camera. At around midday, Tom, the skipper, lets us know there is a change in the weather approaching. The weather changes and the sea becomes choppy. We pack up and leave the reef at about 2 pm.

sea dragon

Email Files System Applications Help

Inbox 42
Reply
Send
Sent
Seen

From Mark
To Back on land
Subject Allison, Dan, William, Emily
5 attachments

Hi guys,

Now the hard work begins. We must study and run tests on the many samples we collected out in the field. After that, we will begin to compile, analyse and organise our research.

Please email me with your findings because we'll need to start writing up our reports soon.

Thanks!

Mark
Team Leader
Reef Research and Rescue

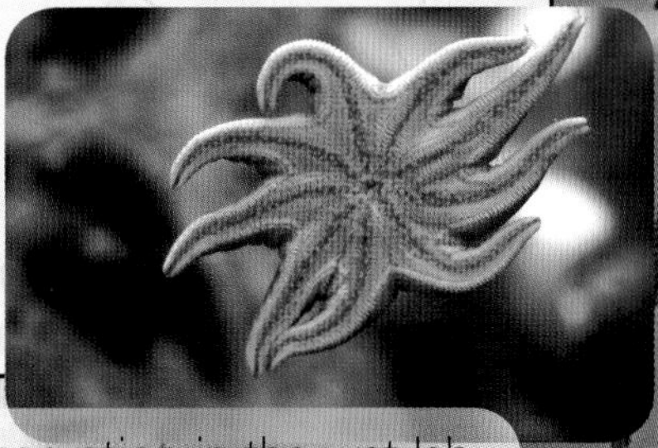

observation in the wet lab

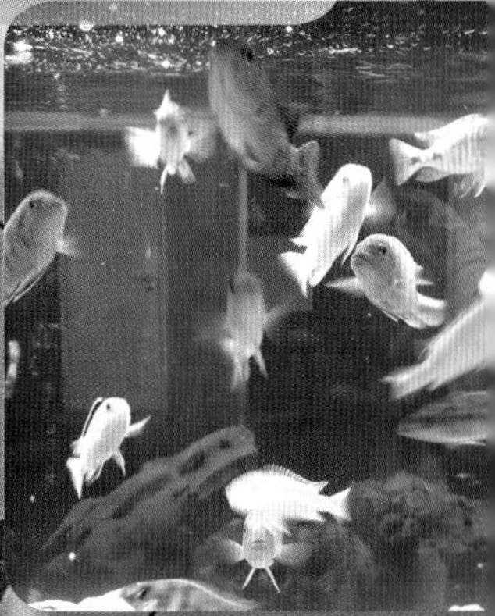

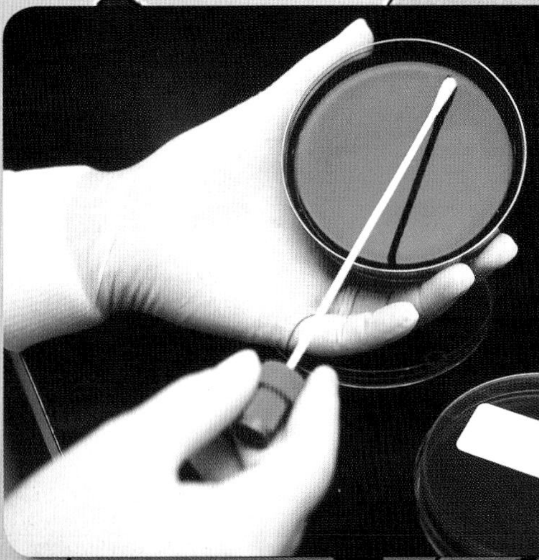

Working carefully with samples is an important part of the job.

When scientists compile research, they must look at the work with an open mind. It is important not to be biased by what you feel, but instead draw your conclusions from proven fact.

The Reef Research and Rescue Centre has two types of laboratories – dry and wet labs. The dry lab is filled with basic scientific equipment like microscopes and computers to conduct experiments and record findings. There is also video and camera imaging equipment and an array of specialised machines to carry out advanced testing.

The wet lab has all kinds of tanks and fridges for holding samples and conducting experiments. It also has a tank that houses a living reef. Tens of thousands of litres of sea water are continuously circulating through the tank's filters. The room is temperature and light controlled.

This is where we transfer our live coral fish, weed samples and invertebrates. We monitor their life cycles, feeding habits and other details in the controlled environment of the wet lab.

Science lab 2 – where we carry out our research.

Our specimens in the fridge – everything must be stored properly.

DIDYOUKNOW?

Pure or applied?
There are two kinds of scientific research:

- pure research – which looks for new knowledge in a certain area
- applied research – which tries to solve specific real-life problems

Email | Files | System | Applications | Help

Inbox 42

Reply

Send

Sent

Seen

From Mark
To Findings from our research
Subject Malcome de Mer MP
4 attachments

Dear Mal,

One month after our return, we are still gathering the results of our research from the trip. Some of the experiments are ongoing but the information gathered so far is enough for each team member to present his or her findings. Here is a brief update:

Emily found fish numbers were strong and there was a healthy biodiversity of fish on the reef. Plankton levels were good for maintaining such fish populations. This reef is part of an area in the Great Barrier Reef where fishing is banned. Fish numbers in areas closer to the coast, where fishing is still allowed, show less diversity and only a third of the fish numbers found on this reef.

We thank you for your continued interest in the conservation of the marine park.
Please see the attachments for some of the pressing issues.

Your sincerely,

Mark Dawson
Team Leader
Reef Research and Rescue

Marine biologists may have found a new form of first aid for injured reefs. Researchers at the University of Guam have managed to grow ten species of coral. They hope this could lead to aquarium suppliers 'farming' coral. Live patches of farmed coral could be applied to damaged reefs, helping them to regenerate. There could then be a bank of corals to transplant into damaged reefs all over the world.

Keeping up fish numbers depends on protected areas.

coral colonies affected by rapid temperature change

Can reef-building corals adapt or acclimatise to these rapid climate changes?

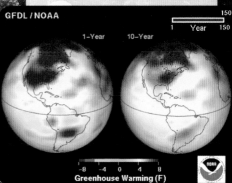

GFDL / NOAA

150
1 Year 150

1–Year   10–Year

-8   -4   0   4   8
Greenhouse Warming (F)

LOSING NEMO

The film, Finding Nemo, made us (the clownfish) so famous that suddenly everyone wanted us in their fish tanks at home. We are now at risk of extinction in Thai ocean waters because of the great demand for us as pets.

Some fish hunters even resort to using poisonous chemicals that make all the fish in the water pass out and float to the surface. The desired fish are then plucked from the top of the water. Many of the fish left in the ocean never recover from the poison.

A large clownfish may live for over 100 years.

If a clownfish leaves its anemone for 24 hours or more, when it returns it has to build up its immunity to the sting all over again!

To cope with the situation, the Krabi Coastal Aquaculture Centre and the Department of Fisheries in Thailand started a breeding programme in 2000 in an attempt to save the real Nemo and increase its numbers. The centre has been successful in breeding seven species of anemone fish (the clownfish) found in the Andaman Sea and the Gulf of Thailand.

Some fish from the centre are sold directly to fish shops. Others are released into the ocean, but only on the condition that people living in the area protect the fish from poachers. So far, fish have been released around the Phi Phi islands and in the sea near the Krabi province.

In the future, scientists plan to breed other kinds of popular aquarium fish that are on the brink of extinction.

All clownfish begin life as males. If the female of a breeding pair disappears, the male will become female and a young male will take his place.

TO DO

SEND information to professional journals, government departments, universities, the media, other marine biologists and the Internet.

Our research findings

Dan found the coral, in general, was very healthy. Further tests showed that water quality was excellent for coral growth to continue. There was little evidence of coral bleaching.

There were a number of crown-of-thorns starfish recorded in the field area, but not at major damage numbers. We will continue to monitor their numbers.

Allison found there was a wide range of plant life. She discovered some very interesting results about the nutrition and chemistry of some algae species. Her research into these issues is ongoing.

William found more than 15 different types of invertebrates in the field area. The sea worms he brought back from the dive have settled in well and are thriving in the wet lab reef. He is still conducting experiments on their feeding habits.

Overall, we found this area of the reef to be in good-to-excellent condition. There was little or no evidence of coral bleaching, coral disease or crown-of-thorns starfish damage. Human impact on this section of the reef has been minimal. To make sure this situation continues, the area has been marked as part of an ongoing yearly monitoring programme.

Where does all the information go?

Once our research has been compiled and organised, it is time to put it into documents, tables and graphs and present it so that others can see the results too.

Marine biologists spend a lot of time writing about their research findings, both to let others know about what they have found and to apply for grants for further research.

Marine biologists usually work normal office hours, but specific projects may mean extra hours. Longer hours are especially likely on field trips at sea, where research must be fitted in around the weather. Field trips may involve being away for long periods, often in uncomfortable conditions.

DIDYOUKNOW?

How deep?

The Mariana Trench, in the Pacific Ocean near Japan, is the deepest part of the ocean we know about. At its deepest, it's 11 kilometres (or 6.9 miles) to the bottom. That's further under the water than the top of Mount Everest is above it!

CORAL

ALGAE

MARINE WEED

SEA WORMS

DIDYOUKNOW?

Money facts

Newly-qualified marine biologists may earn around £17,000 to £20,000 a year.

Asterias
Sea Star

Brittle Star

Echinocardium sp
Sand Dollar

Cucumaria sp
Sea Cucumber

Sea Urchin

ECHINODERM COMPARISON

Follow these steps to become a marine biologist

School subjects you need to study to become a marine biologist:

Maths – for all those statistics!

English – to write and present reports. Join the debating team for practice.

Biology – the foundation of it all.

Chemistry – this will help the biology make sense.

(Physics is an optional subject for this career, but it would be a huge advantage.)

- You will usually need two A levels/three H grades and five GCSE's/S grades (A-C/1-3), or equivalent qualifications.
- Biology is essential at A level/H grade. Maths and another science subject are extremely useful.
- Technological subjects or foreign languages may also help.

Ask your Connexions PA, careers adviser or teacher for more information.

Then at university, some combination of:

Marine science or biology
Botany
Ecology

Fish biology
Marine mammalogy
Conservation courses

- Some people take a degree in marine biology or oceanography. These subjects are offered by a number of universities across the UK.
- It is also possible to do a degree in any of the biological sciences and then go on to specialise in marine biology with a Masters or PhD.

Entrants for research posts need a relevant degree and usually a postgraduate qualification.

Degree courses in marine biology usually involve a combination of lectures, laboratory sessions and fieldwork. On some courses, students spend a year gaining hands-on experience of marine work with a company or laboratory.

Technician support

A possible alternative route is to seek a job providing technical support to scientists. You would still need good exam results but not a degree. After some years' experience, it may be possible to become directly involved in research.

Other useful skills:

- scuba diving experience or qualifications
- first aid qualifications
- boat handling and engine maintenance experience
- displaying care and sensitivity for all animals and plant life
- an ability to respond quickly to unexpected events
- a driving licence
- a boat licence

DIDYOUKNOW?

Who's who in the world of fish

There are more than 250 different species in Welsh seas alone. Our marine biologists have been busy identifying and recording the fish. There is a fish recording website to help fishermen, sea anglers, divers and sailors to record the fish species they have seen or caught. This allows biologists to track changes the fish population and track the arrival of new and unusual species.

 ## Red-hot fact!

It's important to get as much experience as you can through work experience or volunteering but it's difficult if you are under 18. Join the Marine Conservation Society which organises beach cleans and fundraisers. You could also keep a journal of interesting marine facts.

Opportunities for marine biologists

After graduating, you can work for the government, private laboratories, Environmental Protection Agencies and consultancy organisations. There may also be jobs in zoos, rescue centres or aquariums. After gaining experience, some marine biologists set up their own consultancies, or work freelance. There may be opportunities to work abroad.

There are also opportunities for Marine Biology graduates in pharmaceutical and biotechnological companies, bioinformatics, health and clinical sciences, medical science, forensic science and marketing.

Keep up to date

Once qualified, it is important to keep up to date with new developments and learn further skills. The Marine Biological Association runs advanced courses on specific areas of marine science.

Other related careers include:

- Biologist
- Diver
- Ecologist
- Environmental Scientist
- Oceanographer
- Research Scientist
- Zoologist
- Marine Engineering

Useful contacts

Interesting information about marine biology and careers can be found at:

The Marine Biological Association of the United Kingdom (MBA)
www.mba.ac.uk

National Oceanography Centre www.soc.soton.ac.uk

Marine Conservation Society UK and Scotland www.mcsuk.org

Natural Environment Research Council (NERC) www.nerc.ac.uk

The Centre for Environment, Fisheries and Aquaculture Science (CEFAS) www.cefas.co.uk

Challenger Society for Marine Science www.challenger-society.org.uk

Fisheries Research Services www.marlab.ac.uk

Institute of Biology www.iob.org

The Scottish Association for Marine Science www.sams.ac.uk

Society for Underwater Technology (SUT) www.sut.org.uk

The **UCAS** website gives details of all marine biology, oceanography and related degree courses www.ucas.ac.uk

Glossary

algae – photosynthesising organisms found in or near water, ranging from single cells to giant kelp; not plants – do not have roots, stems, leaves or flowers

biologist – a scientist who studies living things

botanist – a scientist who specifically studies plants

carbon dioxide – a natural gas produced by animals breathing which is absorbed by plants

crustacean – marine invertebrate with a soft, segmented body and a hard, segmented shell, with pairs of jointed legs, e.g. lobster

data – information gained from studying or monitoring something

ecosystem – a community of organisms interacting with each other and their environment

GPS – Global Positioning System – a satellite navigational system which is used to calculate position

invertebrate – animal without a backbone

krill – tiny, shrimp-like ocean crustaceans which live in large swarms; the main food of the blue whale

mammalogy – a branch of zoology that studies mammals

mollusc – marine invertebrate with a soft, unsegmented body enclosed in a hard shell, e.g. snail

nutrients – anything taken in or eaten by living things

organism – any individual living animal or plant

plankton – microscopic plants and animals that drift in the ocean; form the start of most marine food chains

polyp – tiny, column-like animal which makes up coral

regulator – scuba diving device which controls and changes air pressure

sediment – materials such as sand, gravel and clay carried along by water; dregs which settle at the bottom of a liquid

zoologist – a scientist who specifically studies animals

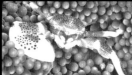

Index

other titles in the series

PILOT

FORENSIC SCIENTIST

TV PRODUCER

MAGAZINE EDITOR

GAME DEVELOPER

MOTOR MECHANIC

ANIMATOR

BUILDER

CHEF

SPORTS TRAINER

FASHION DESIGNER

CHOREOGRAPHER

ZOO KEEPER

FIRE FIGHTER

LAWYER